INTERACTIVE **WORKBOOK**

COURAGE TO SPEAK™

Blasting the Barriers of Silence

Thank you to Theresa Harvard Johnson for your contribution to *Courage to Speak*.

BOOKLOGIX

Alpharetta, GA

The resources contained within this book are provided for informational purposes only and should not be used to replace the specialized training and professional judgment of a healthcare or mental healthcare professional. Angela's Voice and the publisher of this work cannot be held responsible for the use of the information provided. Always consult a licensed mental health professional before making any decision regarding treatment of yourself or others.

Copyright © 2013, 2023 by Angela's Voice

Second Edition

All rights reserved. No part of this book may be reproduced or transmitted in any form or by any means, electronic or mechanical, including photocopying, recording, or any information storage and retrieval system, without permission in writing from the author.

ISBN: 978-1-61005-990-9

This ISBN is the property of BookLogix for the express purpose of sales and distribution of this title. The content of this book is the property of the copyright holder only. BookLogix does not hold any ownership of the content of this book and is not liable in any way for the materials contained within. The views and opinions expressed in this book are the property of the Author/Copyright holder, and do not necessarily reflect those of BookLogix.

∞ This paper meets the requirements of ANSI/NISO Z39.48-1992 (Permanence of Paper)

Workbook text and editing by Theresa Harvard Johnson, Angela Williams.
Design and Illustration by Mark Sandlin.
Design production by Felicia Kahn.

050923

CONTENTS

Barriers to Change 1

No Unified Definition for Child Sexual Abuse 2

No Unified Tracking, Reporting or Recording of Data on a National Scale 5

Societal Denial 7

Inadequate Punishment 10

The Devastating Effects of a Silent Society 15

    Training a Vigilant Society 17

    The Front Line of a Vigilant Society 19

    A Code of Silence Among Survivors 21

Developing Environments that Promote Disclosure 23

Gaining the Courage to Speak 25

Celebrating Disclosure 26

Angela's Voice 28

Join the Angela's Voice Movement 30

BARRIERS TO CHANGE

There are many barriers to understanding and dealing with the growing epidemic of child sexual abuse. This is a global issue that is devastating, socially destructive and, in some ways, ambiguous in that there are no definitive strategies in place to eradicate the problem.

What is equally alarming is this realization: Nations, including the United States, have not (1) established a unified definition of what child sexual abuse is; (2) adequately or accurately tracked, captured or recorded data concerning child sexual abuse or coordinated strategic efforts to do so; (3) initiated or launched substantial and consistent efforts to awaken society to this increasingly violent and growing epidemic; (4) established laws that allow the punishment to fit the severity of the crime; (5) trained a vigilant society against child sexual abuse by facilitating child sexual abuse educational prevention programs and resources, or (6) created environments that support disclosure and healing for the survivor.

In other words, our national stand against child sexual abuse is still unclear and sporadic at best. Our greatest challenge in this hour is breaking down these barriers that block decisive progress and immediate action to protect our children against this type of abuse. The message conveyed must be one of no tolerance. If these barriers fail to come down, communities worldwide run the risk of propagating a societal message that devalues our children and minimizes their need to be fiercely protected. If we unite as a nation to remove these barriers, we stand at the brink of ending these horrific crimes against our children and giving them the "COURAGE TO SPEAK."

Let's take a detailed look at the six obstacles to change as they relate to the United States.

NO UNIFIED DEFINITION FOR CHILD SEXUAL ABUSE

As a society, there is an ongoing need to have a unified and working definition of child sexual abuse – one that is so defined that there are no misconceptions or confusing assumptions concerning what it looks like or the traumatic impact it has on children. As it stands now, the term child sexual abuse could mean molestation to some and child rape to others. In truth, the definition includes both of these as well as a wide range of abuses and assaults. Having a clear definition as we continue to research this issue and gain understanding about the best ways to protect our children ensures that there are no misunderstandings, miscommunications or confusion that would impede progress. It would potentially set a standard by which all tracking, data collection and data interpretation could be measured and disseminated. *(We will expound on this further in the next section.)* This step is critical.

Dr. David Finkelhor, director of the Crimes Against Children Research Center and a renowned expert on this issue, noted in his speech at the Penn State Child Sexual Abuse Conference in 2012 that there has been poor coordination among key institutions in our country concerning data tracking, collection and defining the problem of child sexual abuse. Finkelhor stated that part of the problem is that the issue of child sexual abuse "is spread across a number of different institutional domains that don't work well together and have not coordinated"[1] their efforts. The largest organization he identified was the child protection agency, and he noted that while they report solid data in the areas they target and use the terminology *child sexual abuse*, "the numbers they account for are only for caregivers in the home environment and do not include stats outside of this."[2] In other words, they specifically capture data on children who are sexually abused in homes with caregivers. All other data – outside of that environment – is excluded.

Finkelhor also stated that we have a "criminal justice system that doesn't use the term"[3] sexual abuse in its descriptions. He noted that the criminal justice system's major crime

---

[1] Finkelhor, Ph.D, David, dir. *PSU Child Sexual Abuse Conference: Overview and Epidemiology.* 2012. Web. 5 Mar 2013. <http://www.youtube.com/watch?v=G-fViw7Uuxs&feature=youtu.be>.
[2] Ibid.
[3] Ibid.

reporting system – the Federal Bureau of Investigation, the National Crime Victim Survey and the Uniformed Crime Reporting System – is based on victimization in which they do not count child sexual abuse cases separately or report the number of children involved in the crimes; but they do count forcible rape and sexual assault. In addition, he noted that they use terms like "indecent liberties, gross sexual misconduct and a whole bunch of criminal justice gibberish"[4] that makes it difficult to match up with terms like sexual abuse. Let's take a look at some practical examples of existing definitions from leading agencies.

The Centers for Disease Control defines sexual abuse this way:

> "Child sexual abuse involves any sexual activity with a child where consent is not or cannot be given. This includes sexual contact that is accompanied by force or threat, regardless of age of participants, and all sexual contact between an adult and a child, regardless of whether or not there is deception or the child understands the sexual nature of the activity. Sexual contact between an older and younger child can also be abusive if there is significant disparity in age, development, or size, rendering the younger child incapable of giving informed consent. The sexually abusive acts may include sexual penetration, sexual touching, or non-contact sexual acts such as voyeurism or exhibitionism."[5]

The American Psychological Association defines sexual abuse in these terms:

> "Child sexual abuse is any interaction between a child and adult (or another child) in which the child is used for the sexual stimulation of the perpetrator or observer. A central characteristic of abuse is the domination of a child by the perpetrator through deception, force, or coercion into sexual activity. Children, due to their age, cannot give meaningful consent to sexual activity. Child sexual abuse includes touching and non-touching behaviors like sexual kissing; inappropriate touching or fondling of the child's genitals, breasts or buttocks; masturbation; oral-genital contact; sexual or digital (with fingers) penetration; pornography (forcing the child to view or use of the child in); child prostitution; exposure or flashing of body parts to a child; voyeurism (ogling a child) or verbal pressure for sex."[6]

---

4   Ibid.
5   Saul, Ph.D., Janet, and Natalie Audage, Ph.D. United States Department of Health & Human Services. Centers for Disease Control and Prevention. *Preventing Child Sexual Abuse Within Youth Serving Organizations: Getting Started on Policies and Procedures*. Atlanta: National Center for Injury Prevention Control, 2007. Print.
6   "Child Sexual Abuse: What parents should know." *American Psychological Association*. American Psychological Association, 8 Apr 2010. Web. 5 Mar 2013. <http://www.apa.org/pi/families/resources/child-sexual-abuse.asp&xgt;.

The United States National Library of Health and National Institutes of Health define child sexual abuse using this terminology: "Child sexual abuse is the deliberate exposure of minor children to sexual activity. This means a child is forced or talked into sex or sexual activities by another person. Such abuse includes: oral sex, pornography, sexual intercourse, touching (fondling)."[7] Now, take a very close look at these definitions – note their similarities and differences. Then consider this fact: Not only do definitions concerning child sexual abuse vary by governmental entities and professional organizations, but the *legal or criminal* definitions of child sexual abuse vary by state when sexual contact "occurs between a minor (someone under 18 years of age) and someone 5 or more years older."[8] What does this mean? It means that each state has been given the responsibility to determine how child sexual abuse is defined. Clearly, we can now see how our nation would benefit from a concise definition. It is our position in writing this workbook, *Courage to Speak,* that aggressive, coordinated efforts are needed to develop a working definition that accurately, clearly and explicitly defines child sexual abuse in such a way that it sets a precedent globally. In addition, other terms associated with child sexual abuse could also be clearly defined including pedophile, pedophilia, child sexual predators, grooming, child molester, child molestation, aggravated child molestation, etc.

For Further Reflection:

1. What did you learn in this section that was most surprising to you?

_____
_____
_____

2. What terms are you still unsure of?

_____
_____
_____

---

[7] Zieve, MD, MHA, David Eltz, eds. "Child abuse - sexual." *MedlinePlus: Health Information for You.* U.S. National Library of Medicine, National Institutes of Health, 17 Sep 2012. Web. 5 Mar 2013. <http://www.nlm.nih.gov/medlineplus/ency/article/007224.htm>.

[8] Cruise, Ph.D., Tracy K. "Sexual Abuse of Children and Adolescents." *National Association of School Psychologists.* Bethesda: 2004. <http://www.nasponline.org/educators/sexualabuse.pdf>.

NO UNIFIED TRACKING, REPORTING OR RECORDING OF DATA ON A NATIONAL SCALE

In the previous section, we briefly discussed data from a speech given by Finkelhor at the Penn State University conference on child sexual abuse. We looked at the problems with data tracking, collection and reporting between key agencies. Let's take a closer look.

Finkelhor warned that a number of key data collection systems currently used by these leading organizations were set up prior to the years when concerns about child sexual abuse began to rise to the forefront and are outdated. As a result, these agencies have not set up criteria either to capture child sexual abuse or to put systems in place to store such data.

In a document published in 2000 by multi-government agencies including the United States Department of Justice, the Federal Bureau of Investigation, the Criminal Justice Information Services Division, and the Uniform Crime Reporting Program, the recommendations for guidelines and specifications used in the National Incident Based Reporting system were set forth in a web-based document titled the *"National Incident Based-Reporting System Volume I: Data Collection Guidelines."* The following statement is from page one of this document:

> "The guidelines and specifications used in NIBRS are based on the recommendations of Abt Associates Inc., as set forth in their report entitled Blueprint for the Future of the Uniform Crime Reporting Program, dated May 1985. Using the Blueprint's recommendations for general guidance, in January 1986 a private contractor and the FBI's Technical Services Division were assigned the task of developing the guidelines and design specifications for implementing a new incident-based system. Overall direction of the project was performed by the FBI's UCR staff.
>
> Advice was sought and received from the Association of State UCR Programs, International Association of Chiefs of Police, National Sheriffs' Association, National

Alliance of State Drug Enforcement Agencies, Drug Enforcement Administration, and various local, state, and federal criminal justice agencies. This collaboration was accomplished through formal conferences, informal meetings, and written and telephone contacts. The advice received was of invaluable assistance in the preparation and refinement of the guidelines and specifications."[9]

What does this mean? Well, it means that our national data collection systems have not been updated in nearly 30 years. It also presents a good picture of the interagency effort and the tremendous financial expense that went into developing this now outdated data collection system. In addition, it shows the type of data that these agencies currently collect which include motor vehicle theft, credit card fraud, arson and murder and data on sexual offenses – but no data on child sexual abuse.

In simple terms, this means that our nation lacks coordinated and uniform initiatives to track, collect, and report data necessary for developing processes to reveal the severity of child sexual abuse and present relevant solutions to our fight against it. To date, there are no widely published plans or efforts in place to begin overhauling our data reporting systems on a wide-scale national level.

Now, let's put all of this in perspective so that anyone can understand what is being conveyed here. In Finkelhor's presentation, it is noted that as a nation we have data supporting how many people have contracted obscure diseases like Cholera, Powassan virus disease, St. Louis encephalitis disease, Q fever and more than 60 other infectious diseases. The Penn State presentation notes that data is also collected on the number of young people injured on farm machinery and how many people have been bitten by the brown recluse spider. Yet, in comparison to the data collected on rather obscure and/or infrequent occurrences, no specific research is available to address child sexual abuse at this level, nor has there been significant funding set aside to launch a unified national effort to do so. This is significant because it shows that finances, personnel and countless hours are being invested by government agencies to research and record data in areas that are not known or even of interest to the average person while very few of these resources have been placed into protecting our children from sexual abuse.

---

9   United States, Washington, DC. The Federal Bureau of Investigation, The Department of Justice. *National Incident Based-Reporting System Volume I: Data Collection Guidelines*. Washington, DC , 2000. Web. <http://www.fbi.gov/about-us/cjis/ucr/nibrs/nibrs_dcguide.pdf>.

> For Further Reflection
>
> 1. Why is the collection of data on child sexual abuse essential?
> _____
> _____
>
> 2. Why is interagency cooperation and communication a necessary tool in the fight against child sexual abuse?
> _____
> _____

SOCIETAL DENIAL

Briefly, read this excerpt from the article *"Running Away from Child Sexual Abuse: Denial Revisited,"* by May Benartar, Ph.D:

> "After a period of increased professional and public awareness of how pervasive the sexual maltreatment of children is in our society, we appear to be in danger of vaulting away from hard-won insights into this major public health issue. Both propounding and expressing the prejudices of the culture, the press and other media have taken to indicting the veracity of traumatic memories of survivors of sexual abuse, minimizing the toxic long-term effects of the sexual maltreatment of children, and casting doubt on both the skill and good intentions of clinicians treating both child victims and adult survivors. We have seen front-page articles on the purported 'false' memories of adult survivors of abuse; examples of 'false' accusations of innocent parents, grandparents, or teachers; or speculations that therapists, many of whom are survivors themselves, intentionally or unintentionally suggest events to their patients that never took place."[10]

---

10 Benatar, May. "Running Away from Sexual Abuse: Denial." *Families in Society* 76.5 (1995): 315-. ProQuest Central. Web. 6 Mar. 2013. Revisited

This excerpt from Benatar's article provides a glimpse of what societal denial of child sexual abuse might look like in the media. In her full article, she cited numerous publications and broadcasts that influence our society and identified key messages that minimize or even dismiss the validity and seriousness of this heinous crime. All of which, she suggests, contributes to creating a society that denies the reality of just how devastating and prevalent child sexual abuse is in our culture. According to Dr. Tara Ney, author of *True and False Allegations of Child Sexual Abuse*, in 1976 only 6,000 cases of child sexual abuse were reported and in 1993 this number had increased 55 percent to 300,000. Of that number, 2 to 8 percent were false allegations.[11]

Child sexual abuse denial, therefore, can be defined as refusing to acknowledge that the issue really exists. This is another significant boulder that creates barriers of societal denial that makes it increasingly difficult to protect our children from sexual predators.

Benatar challenges readers with this statement:

"The reality of child abuse is well established. Why then is it currently acceptable, even fashionable, to doubt the victims, those who prosecute for them, and those who treat their post-traumatic illnesses? This backlash against sexual-abuse survivors has social, cultural, political, and psychological roots. One reading is that this backlash is a response to the evolution in law regarding the issue of incest--an evolution that now allows some adult survivors to seek legal redress many years, even decades, after the commission of crimes. On another level of analysis, we may understand this phenomenon of denial of social realities as 'cultural dissociation.' As a society we are unable to accept the reality of the cruelty, sadism, neglect, and narcissism that adults inflict upon children. In a world where some people still debate the reality of Nazi death camps, it is not surprising that we have difficulties acknowledging that 1 of every 3 girls and perhaps 1 of 7 to 10 boys are 'used' by an adult in a manner that brings great harm to them for the rest of their lives."[12]

---

11   Ney, Ph.D., Tara. *True and False Allegations of Child Sexual Abuse*. New York: Brunner/Mazel, Inc., 1995. (accessed April 10, 2013).
12   Ibid.

Benatar used the term "cultural dissociation" in the passage above. Dissociation is a term used in psychology to describe the process of "detaching" one's mind from a mental or physical experience and completely stepping outside of reality. The detachment can be mild or extreme and allows one to completely depersonalize, minimize and pay little attention to that experience. In this specific instance, we can define *cultural* dissociation as a societal environment that has detached or separated itself from the reality of child sexual abuse. It has split off into an alternate reality that says, "It's not really as bad as everyone says it is."

In 1994, Finkelhor stated that "as reports of sexual abuse have increased and particularly as some cases with false or questionable accusations have been widely publicized, some observers have alleged that the country is caught up in a hysteria of sexual abuse accusations and prosecutions."[13] Yet in an October 2012 article entitled "Boy Scout Files Give Glimpse Into 20 Years of Sex Abuse", The New York Times reporter Kirk Johnson wrote, "Details of decades of sexual abuse in the Boy Scouts of America, and what child welfare experts say was a *corrosive culture of secrecy* that compounded the damage, were cast into full public view for the first time on Thursday with the release of thousands of pages of documents describing abuse accusations across the country."[14]

Now, take a look at what Finkelhor wrote about the societal view of some pertaining to child sexual abuse and what is actually revealed in the case reported by Johnson. These contrasts paint a clear picture of what societal denial can look like. Even though the tragedy of the offenses concerning Boy Scouts of America has been revealed, the shock-waves seem to have died down and our nation has returned to its sleep-state. Instead, the news of the hour in regard to this organization is on this question: *Should Boy Scouts of America allow gay members?* Can you see the denial – this quick shifting or refocusing of issues?

A form of denial can also be seen by parents who fear that they are raping the minds of their children by making them aware of the reality of child sexual abuse. In other words, they are more concerned with their children being made aware of the possibility of sexual

---

13 Finkelhor, Ph.D., David. "Current Information on the Scope and Nature of Child Sexual Abuse." *The Future of Children*. 2. Durham: 1994. <http://www.unh.edu/ccrc/pdf/VS75.pdf>.
14 Johnson, Kirk. "Boy Scout Files Give Glimpse Into 20 Years of Sex Abuse." *New York Times* [New York] 18 October 2012, A20. Web. 11 Mar. 2013. <http://www.nytimes.com/2012/10/19/us/boy-scout-documents-reveal-decades-of-sexual-abuse.html?pagewanted=all&_r=0>.

violence than they are about protecting them through awareness. This is yet another form of societal denial.

Denial is also the result of ignorance which leads into developing and spreading myths. Some of the most common myths concerning child sexual abuse are (1) denying the existence of child sexual abuse or asserting that it is extremely rare; (2) believing that only girls are the ones abused; (3) believing perpetrator stereotypes as it relates to socio economic status, culture or ethnic group; (4) believing that boys are less traumatized than girls; (5) believing that abusers are always strangers (stranger danger), and (6) believing that children are prone to making false accusations.

Remember! When a society is in denial, it will not have a desire to confront the issue or address it on any level that can affect long-term change. To the survivors of child sexual abuse, this denial sends a message to them that no one cares, believes them or will come to their rescue if they have the "COURAGE TO SPEAK." Experts agree that social change and societal awakening must begin with awareness and education that permeates every area of our society from families all the way up to the legislative level.

> For Further Reflection
>
> 1. Which aspect of societal denial applies most to the community you live in?
> _____
> _____
>
> 2. What aspect of child sexual abuse would make it most difficult for you to speak about?
> _____
> _____

INADEQUATE PUNISHMENT

In efforts to help tell her story, Angela's Voice interviewed a woman who was sexually abused by her father for over a decade in a small Georgia town. Her father, who was also a law enforcement official, was prosecuted for child molestation and sentenced to only two years in prison.

She, along with her family, emphatically states that they have received no true justice for all that they have endured.

While stronger penalties have resulted in some child sexual abuse cases over the past two decades, there are many more in which justice has not been served. When examining the sentencing data in US history, it becomes clear that penalties for child sexual abuse are erratic at best. While there has been some progress, we are still without national, unified strategies and resources to address these issues at the depth needed. Take a look at the news headlines below. Note that we fully understand that every case and legal circumstance is as unique as we are as individuals. Our position in presenting this information is simple: *The punishment for any act of child sexual abuse should send a message that as a nation we will not tolerate these types of atrocious, unimaginable crimes against our children.*

NEWS HEADLINES:

- **David Harold Earls: Child Rapist Gets One Year in Plea Deal.**[15] The child was four years old.
- **Kingsbury Man Sentenced to Prison for Child Sexual Abuse (3 Years).**[16] The children were 10, 14 and 16.
- **Convicted child rapist receives 3 life sentences.**[17] The child was 9 years old.
- **Oberlin child rapist, 70, gets 13 years; young victim reads letter explaining hurt, terror.**[18] The child was 13 years old.
- **Retired Orange County Priest Sentenced in Molestation Case.**[19] He was sentenced to 400 hours of community service. The child was abused between the ages of 7 and 9.

---

15 Murphy, Sean. " David Harold Earls: Child Rapist Gets One Year In Plea Deal." *Huffington Post.* 16 Jun 2009: Web. 11 Mar. 2013. <http://www.huffingtonpost.com/2009/06/17/david-harold-earls-child-_n_217034.html>.

16 "Kingsbury man sentenced to prison for child sexual abuse." *PostStar.* 7 May 2013: Web. 11 Mar. 2013. <http://poststar.com/news/blotter/kingsbury-man-sentenced-to-prison-for-child-sexual-abuse/article_e13b038e-8731-11e2-b62e-0019bb2963f4.html>.

17 "Convicted child rapist receives 3 life sentences." *FOX19.com* [Hamilton] 15 March 2012, Web. 15 Mar. 2013. <http://www.fox19.com/story/17164776/convicted-child-rapist-faces-sentencing>.

18 Remington, Kaylee. "Oberlin child rapist, 70, gets 13 years; young victim reads letter explaining hurt, terror." *Morning Journal* [Oberline] 5 February 2013, Web. 16 Mar. 2013. <http://www.morningjournal.com/articles/2013/02/05/news/doc51108c682c084476699317.txt>.

19 Kandel, Jason. "Retired Orange County Priest Sentenced in Molestation Case." *NBC Southern California* [Los Angeles] 24 August 2012, Web. 16 Mar. 2013. <http://www.nbclosangeles.com/news/local/Denis-Lyons-Retired-Catholic-Priest-Orange-County-Costa-Mesa-Sexual-Assault-167347935.html>.

In an article published by ForbesWoman Magazine, reporter Wendy J. Murphy wrote this concerning the Penn State University Scandal penalty: "The loss of a few college bowl games, a $90 million dollar fine and stripping the late Joe Paterno of his status as the winningest coach in history aren't enough. The National Collegiate Athletic Association's recent sanctions against Penn State don't fit the crime *given how much harm was done to so many victims.* The systematic abuse of children should have caused long-term pain for a university that knowingly allowed Jerry Sandusky to use Penn State as a virtual torture chamber."[20] Murphy accurately captures the primary point we are highlighting in this section.

The Department of Psychology at the University of Toledo published the following findings in the 2000 Child Abuse & Neglect journal. The findings will confirm our position on this issue and shed light on our nation's progress in this area over the last 25 to 35 years. An excerpt reads:

> "The study compares criminal penalties for perpetrators of child sexual abuse (CSA) and adult sexual assault (ASA) between 1980 and 1985. CSA and ASA sentences were compared in 3 counties in 3 different states. Alleged child sexual abuse perpetrators experienced fewer prosecutions and convictions, less incarceration time, and more probation for child sexual abuse as compared to alleged offenders against adults. More CSA offenders plead guilty (73%) than adult victim cases (67%). The researchers believe that this is the result of prosecutors ensuring they have extremely strong cases before going to court. They also state that slightly over one third of CSA offenders received short sentences of no more than 5 months and at least 10% received a sentence of 1 month. Fifty-five percent of CSA offenders received 12 months or less with 18% receiving more than a 10 year sentence. In contrast, 39% ASA offenders receive longer sentences of more than 10 years, while 23% of adult offenders received sentences of one year or less. Offenders were sentenced to probation nearly twice as often in CSA as ASA. Familiarity with the abuser was more common in CSA, yet only 19% of the offenders in CSA cases were issued 'no contact' orders from the court. Mandatory counseling was issued in almost half of the CSA cases as compared to only 13% of adult cases."[21]

---

20   Murphy, Wendy J. "Penn State Sanctions Too Little, But Good Start." *Forbes Woman Magazine*. 28 Aug 2013: Web. 11 Mar. 2013. <http://www.forbes.com/sites/womensenews/2012/08/28/penn-state-sanctions-too-little-but-good-start/>.
21   Cullen, Bernard, et al. "A matched cohort comparison of a criminal justice system's response to child sexual abuse: a profile of perpetrators." *Child Abuse & Neglect*. Volume 24.4 (2000): 569 - 577 . Web. 16 Mar. 2013. <http://www.ncbi.nlm.nih.gov/pubmed/10798845>.

The information compiled is this journal is confounding, and clearly shows the historical backdrop that outlines the work to prevent child sexual abuse over the last several decades. What is even more alarming is knowing that billions of dollars, research and resources have gone into cracking down on drug offenses, often imposing mandatory life sentences for *first-time offenders*. When reviewing research in this area, even casually, you will quickly learn that the penalties for sexually abusing a child can barely be compared.

A New York Times article reported, "Three decades of stricter drug laws, reduced parole and rigid sentencing rules have lengthened prison terms and more than tripled the percentage of Americans behind bars."[22] According to the Office of National Drug Policy Control, $15 billion was spent in 2010 on the war on drugs, and for $10 billion to drug education alone this year.

Efforts to bring House Bill 3650, "Federal Zero Tolerance of Child Sexual Abuse Act of 2011" to life failed. The bill would have prevented institutions of higher education and nonprofit organizations that fail to report incidents of sexual abuse of a minor from receiving Federal funds. This would have marked a huge hit to the budget of institutions like Penn State and would have assisted in sending out a profound and clear message that we will not tolerate the cover up of child sexual abuse or the acts of child sexual abuse in our institutions.

In 2006, legislation passed in Georgia that strengthened "laws protecting children from sexual predators (HB1059)."[23] Enticing a child for indecent purposes previously garnered a sentence between 1-20 years, but under the revised law the penalty rose to 10-30 years. For incest, the sentence was between 1-20 years; under the revised law, it rose to 10-30 years. In addition, the legislation created a new statute that sentences those found guilty of harboring sex offenders to 5-20 years. In 2012 the Georgia Legislature removed the statute of limitations on Child Sexual Abuse Cases and broadened the Mandatory Reporting Laws to include all volunteers working with children. Approximately 107 bills in 30 states and the District of Columbia were introduced in the 2012 legislative session on the reporting of suspected child abuse and neglect; 10 of these states have enacted legislation.

---

22   Tierney, John. "For Lesser Crimes, Rethinking Life Behind Bars." *New York Times* [New York City] 11 December 2012, Science Section. Web. 17 Mar. 2013. <http://www.nytimes.com/2012/12/12/science/mandatory-prison-sentences-face-growing-skepticism.html?pagewanted=all&_r=0>.

23   "Governor Perdue Signs Legislation Strengthening Georgia's Sexual Predator Laws." *Governor Sonny Perdue*. State of Georgia, 26 Apr 2006. Web. 15 Mar 2013. <http://sonnyperdue.georgia.gov/00/press/detail/0,2668,78006749_90413728_91434876,00.html>.

Georgia is one of a number of states that have stepped up efforts over the past two years to strengthen penalties for child sexual abuse. Other cities and states that have made national headlines since 2011 as well include but are not limited to Chicago, Florida, Maine, Oregon, New Jersey, and New York. While these efforts represent some progress, we cannot ignore the present and dire need for a unified, *federal* effort and federal funding to ensure that the punishment for child sexual predators fit their crimes and represent justice for their victims. The lack of adequate penalties for this crime remains an obstacle to overcoming it in our nation.

Picture this:

> We live in a country that has been ranked as having one of the best qualities of life in the world.[24] Forbes magazine also ranks the United States as being among the top 10 richest countries in the world. In addition, various reports still describe the United States, at least for now, as the superpower of the world – meaning the most powerful and influential entity on the planet. If this is the case, our nation should be challenged and hard-pressed to do whatever is necessary to protect its most precious commodity – our children. Our country is, and has been for generations, a trendsetter from technological innovations to lifestyle. It is our position that child sexual abuse is no different. If we can set the stage for issues like the war on drugs and gun safety, how impactful could this country be if this issue was heavily pushed to the forefront. We could set the stage for child protection from sexual abuse globally. Our country has that kind of power and influence on the entire world.

For Further Reflection

1. What does the information on sentencing for sexual crimes against children say about our values as a nation?

_____

_____

2. What kind of efforts have been made in your area to ensure that those who commit crimes against children receive adequate punishment?

_____

_____

---

[24] White, Gregory. "These Countries Have The Best Quality Of Life In The World." New York City. May 4, 2011. http://www.businessinsider.com/oecd-better-life-index-2011-5?op=1.

THE DEVASTATING EFFECTS OF A SILENT SOCIETY

A silent society, as we discuss it here, is one that knows about or witnesses atrocities but says or does nothing to stop them or help the victims. It is a society that is so deeply rooted in fear and denial that it refuses to name crimes, identify perpetrators, protect potential victims, support existing survivors or enter into any type of involvement that would place them personally in a posture of advocacy and/or accountability. As a result, that society remains close-mouthed and action-less, choosing to shut itself away from the reality of child sexual abuse.

In recent months, however, some states have enacted legislation that penalizes individuals, organizations and institutions that witness or have possible evidence of child sexual abuse but fail to report it. While we briefly mentioned this in the previous section by highlighting Georgia legislation, I want to identify another state that made headlines recently.

In October 2012, the State of Florida was credited with legislating and enforcing a mandatory "reporting law" as well. A news broadcast from Florida's WCTV reported the following:

> "The law clarifies that all people have an obligation to report suspected sexual abuse of children, regardless of whether the suspected abuser is a parent, neighbor, friend or stranger. Previously, the state's abuse hotline only took reports about sexual abuse by a child's caregivers. The law, HB 1355, 'Protection of Vulnerable Persons,' also imposes a fine of up to $1 million on any public or private college or university whose administration or law enforcement agency willfully and knowingly fails to report child abuse that occurs on its campus, in any of its facilities, or at/during college or university-sponsored events and functions."[25]

---

25   "Nation's Toughest Child Sex Abuse Reporting Law Takes Effect Today in Florida." WCTV Eyewitness News: WCTV, Tallahassee, 12 Oct 2012. Web. 19 Mar 2013. <http://www.wctv.tv/news/headlines/Nations-Toughest-Sex-Abuse-Reporting-Law-Takes-Effect-Today-in-Florida-172154161.html>.

This legislation provides a glimpse of some progress toward BREAKING THE SILENCE. It is our position that future legislation should be developed on a federal level that creates a punishment that fits the crime. For example, a multi-million dollar institution or enterprise would hardly see a $1 million fine as a true punishment. Similarly, receiving community service or probation is not a stiff enough penalty to deter the behavior.

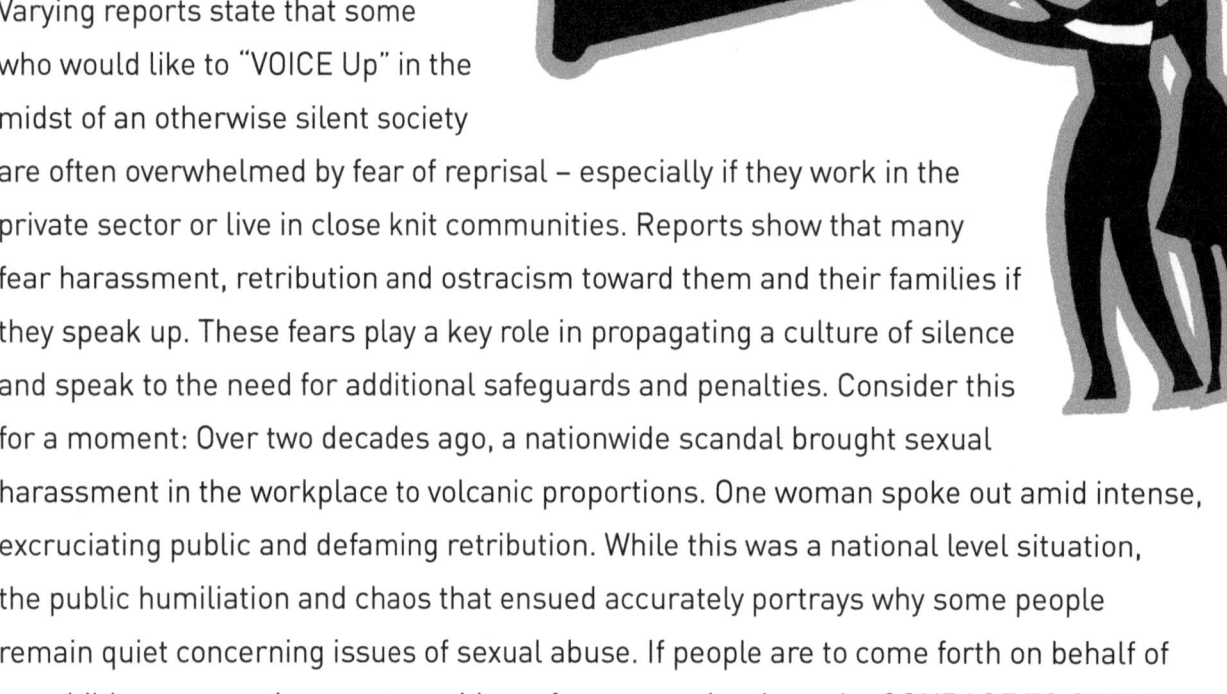

Another point to consider is this: Varying reports state that some who would like to "VOICE Up" in the midst of an otherwise silent society are often overwhelmed by fear of reprisal – especially if they work in the private sector or live in close knit communities. Reports show that many fear harassment, retribution and ostracism toward them and their families if they speak up. These fears play a key role in propagating a culture of silence and speak to the need for additional safeguards and penalties. Consider this for a moment: Over two decades ago, a nationwide scandal brought sexual harassment in the workplace to volcanic proportions. One woman spoke out amid intense, excruciating public and defaming retribution. While this was a national level situation, the public humiliation and chaos that ensued accurately portrays why some people remain quiet concerning issues of sexual abuse. If people are to come forth on behalf of our children, our nation must consider safe ways to give them the COURAGE TO SPEAK. Without their VOICE, survivors will continue to suffer in silence.

A silent society sends a chilling, shocking and equally victimizing message to survivors of child sexual abuse. It says to them:

- ▶ We don't care that this happened to you!
- ▶ We don't believe you!
- ▶ Deal with this on your own!
- ▶ We don't want to expose the perpetrators!
- ▶ Child sexual abuse isn't that big of a deal!
- ▶ Let's pretend this never happened and let's go on with life!

TRAINING A VIGILANT SOCIETY

A vigilant society is one that takes an active role in watching out for and identifying dangers that expose our children to sexual abuse. Experts agree that one of the first steps in training a vigilant society is to prepare or cause its citizens to be acutely aware of the epidemic and its effects, and then arm them in prevention. This workbook, Courage to Speak, is a part of that awakening and awareness.

Silvia M. Dutchevici, MA, LMSW, wrote: "Talking about childhood sexual abuse is difficult. Perhaps, on some level, we believe that if we do not talk about it, it does not exist. Or, perhaps the fact that many cases of childhood sexual abuse often involve incest (where a parent, brother, sister, or relative is the perpetrator) creates an aversion to discussing it. Whatever the reason for our avoidance, in order to stop it, we need to talk about it. We need to allow our friends, co-workers, relatives, and patients to openly discuss the trauma and not suffer in silence. We also need to demand accountability from institutions that are trusted to protect our children, not abuse them."[26]

When our society awakens to the reality of sexual abuse in a similar way that it has awakened to breast cancer awareness or the war on drugs, we will not only begin to see outrage concerning the blatant abuse of our children, but we will also witness prevention efforts in every area of society. This is the end that prevention efforts seek to obtain: *Perpetrators will no longer be able to hide.*

Just as cross-cultural events and activities are initiated to ensure that every woman is aware of the need for a breast exam and every community should alert law enforcement officials to suspected drug activity in their neighborhoods, we need responses for child sexual abuse.

Prevent Child Abuse America's statement summarizes our discussion here: "We, as a nation and as individuals, have the collective responsibility to prevent child sexual abuse. To accomplish this, we must strengthen child abuse prevention services that support children and families. We must enact legislation that protects children from child sexual abuse. And we must promote research, training, and public education to address the risk factors that can lead to child sexual abuse."[27]

---

[26] Dutchevici, MA, LMSW, Sylvia M. "Eliminating the Stigma of Childhood Sexual Abuse." *Good Therapy.org: Helping People Find Therapists & Advocating for Ethical Therapy.* 17 Jul 2012: Online Article. Web. 18 Mar. 2013. <http://www.goodtherapy.org/blog/stigma-childhood-sexual-abuse-0717124>.

[27] "Prevent Child Abuse America." *Preventing Child Sexual Abuse.* PCA America, Web. 18 Mar 2013. <http://www.preventchildabuse.org/advocacy/downloads/child_sexual_abuse.pdf>.

Child sexual abuse affects every area of our society. It has no social or economic class, race, or gender; and any child – boys or girls between the ages of 0 to 18 – could be victimized.

Statistics report that:

- 1 in 4 girls and 1 in 6 boys are sexually abused before the age of 18
- 93 percent of abuse comes from someone a child knows or trusts
- Serial molesters can have up to 400 victims
- Only 1 in 10 will disclose abuse
- There are reportedly 42 million survivors in the United States
- 68 percent of predators sexually abuse children in their own families
- 70 percent of all sexual assaults happen to children under age 17
- 85 percent of men incarcerated for child pornography admit to acting out on a child sexually
- Children with disabilities are at elevated risk of abuse, particularly, if the disability impairs their perceived credibility (blindness, deafness and mental handicap)
- Those with prior history of sexual victimization are extremely likely to be re-victimized.
(Stats were compiled from CDC, APA and PCA America reports.)

The next stat, though it is not specific to child sexual abuse, is critically important in gauging the impact of crimes against children in our society. It shows the impact financially, that child abuse and neglect has on this country from an economic perspective. In a report from the Centers for Disease Control & Prevention, child maltreatment for one year in this country based on "confirmed cases" of child abuse (including physical, psychological abuse, neglect, and sexual abuse) cost survivors and our country "$124 billion annually."[28] In fact, child maltreatment rivals other major health concerns in our country.

---

28   "Cost of Child Abuse and Neglect Rival Other Major Public Health Problems." *CDC*. Centers for Disease Control and Prevention, 1 Feb 2012. Web. 28 Mar 2013. <http://www.cdc.gov/violenceprevention/childmaltreatment/economiccost.html>.

THE FRONT LINE OF A VIGILANT SOCIETY

Experts agree that parents and caregivers are at the frontline when it comes to building a vigilant society. They "are uniquely positioned to assist children who are experiencing sexual violence"[29] and stand at the forefront as their primary protectors. It is critical that the blinders for this segment of society are removed. Parents and caregivers have to face this reality: *All children are at risk of child sexual abuse, and as the statistics have shown, most children are abused by people they know and trust.*

The top three tasks on which parents and caregivers should focus include (1) educating themselves about the warning signs of sexual abuse and identifying sexual predators; (2) talking honestly and openly with children about sex, inappropriate and appropriate behavior beginning at an early age; and (3) engaging other members of society (individuals as well as organizations) concerning child safety as it relates to sexual abuse. Parents and caregivers have a direct line of sight in which they can, with awareness and training, be effective in protecting our children. They also play a key role in creating an environment in which children feel safe enough to disclose. We will discuss this further in the next section.

Also on the frontline are the children themselves. They need the tools to identify uncomfortable and potentially dangerous situations. When it comes to education, we can start as young as three with *age appropriate* activities and teaching moments that paint a clear picture about sex and the risk of sexual abuse. According to Prevent Child Abuse America, "Current child abuse prevention programs are focused primarily on educating preschool and elementary school children how to recognize instances of abuse as well as personal safety skills. Programs may also focus on helping children who are victims of past or ongoing sexual abuse by encouraging them to disclose such incidents to parents or other responsible adults."[30]

---

29 "Informed Adults Play Role In Protecting Children From Sexual Abuse." *The PCAR Pinnacle*. Pennsylvania Coalition Against Rape, 26 Apr 2012. Web. Web. 27 Mar. 2013. <http://www.pcar.org/blog/informed-adults-play-role-protecting-children-sexual-abuse>.
30 Ibid.

While this is a strong place to start, medical professionals and child abuse agencies agree that it is going to take a more comprehensive approach to teaching our children – one that begins in the home with parents and caregivers. In the interactive workbook, *Tough Talk to Tender Hearts*, written and published by Angela's Voice, adults gain practical and age appropriate information about sex and sexual abuse prevention and learn how to communicate this vital information to their children.

The workbook focuses on three primary areas of education:

1. Children need clinical information on the biological process and physiological changes to the body. (This includes making sure they know the anatomy of the body, the correct names for all intimate body parts, their physical functions, changes, etc.)

2. Children need information about sex *at an early age* as a tool against abuse. (Parents should make sure they have "The Talk" with their children, as doing so begins to build trust and open the lines of communication.)

3. Children need information about sex in the context of relationships to introduce the concept of boundaries against abuse and in support of healthy relationships. (For example, a parent would teach that sex is only for adults who love each other, and grownups should have sex only with grownups. When inappropriate information or behavior is presented to them, they may more easily recognize it in the context of the correct behavior taught to them by a parent.)

As the child grows and develops, they become comfortable talking about their anatomy and sex with trusted adults, and mature in their understanding concerning appropriate and inappropriate sexual behaviors. In other words, they will be better equipped to recognize the warning signs when threatened with abuse. This is especially important as we consider our sexually toxic society, and the horrifying fact that many of our children in late elementary and early middle school are engaging in dangerous sex games.

Creating an environment where children can openly ask questions or discuss the reality of sex also builds an environment of trust in which the dangers of child sexual abuse can be discussed, and children will gain the "COURAGE TO SPEAK."

A CODE OF SILENCE AMONG SURVIVORS

Too often, survivors of child sexual abuse suffer in silence – often reaching adulthood before they disclose.

In an article from the Boston Globe, the author wrote: "Cindy was molested by her grandfather when she was 4 years old. When she was 7, she found out from her 8-year-old cousin, Amanda, that their grandfather had molested Amanda as well. Cindy told a counselor years later, 'Neither of us told our mothers because we were afraid to hurt them. Imagine finding out that your father molested your child! We didn't want to get Granddad in trouble, either. We both decided it would be better for the adults if we just kept quiet.'"[31]

Cindy's story isn't uncommon.

In fact, statistics show that only 1 in 10 survivors will tell. Because the abuser is often someone the child knows, they generally have easy access to the child, a position of authority over the child, or a level of control over them. The perpetrators often use coercion to gain and maintain the child's silence and compliance.

A few of the common reasons why children fail to disclose include:

- *Fear of retribution.* The perpetrator will often threaten to harm other family members or even their victims if they tell.
- *Thinking no one will believe them.* Children often think that no one will believe them if they disclose or that they will be branded liars if they tell.
- *Blaming themselves.* Children often blame themselves and harbor feelings of guilt or shame believing they did something to encourage the assault. The abuser can also make the child feel as if he or she was a willing participant.
- *Fear of getting in trouble with their parents or caregivers.* This includes believing that they will be punished if they tell.
- *Fear of destroying the family or their place of community.* This includes being afraid that they will bring hurt to parents or caregivers or being afraid that they will lose key the family relationships and friendships if they disclose. Perpetrators have even threatened to send the children away or otherwise separate them from their families.

---

31   Nancy Benun and, C. B. (1984, May 05). Why children don't tell; sexual abuse victims have learned painful lessons; of obedience, silence and parents' disbelief. *Boston Globe (Pre-1997 Fulltext)*. Retrieved from http://search.proquest.com/docview/294237668?accountid=12085

- *Fear getting their abuser in trouble.* Children may develop guilt or shame after being "groomed" by the perpetrator and developing what they believe to be a close friendship. As a result, they do not want to get the abuser "in trouble." They believe their disclosure equals some sort of betrayal to the relationship.

- *Being bribed into secrecy.* Abusers will also give gifts, trips or special treats if the child "keeps quiet."

In the interactive workbook, *The Grooming Mystery, Unmasking the Predator* written and published by Angela's Voice, patterns of behaviors of a predator are identified.

In a bulletin posted by the American Psychological Association, when survivors suffer in silence they generally endure "fear, anxiety, depression, anger, hostility, aggression, and sexually inappropriate behavior. Frequently reported long-term effects include depression and self-destructive behavior, anxiety, feelings of isolation and stigma, poor self-esteem, difficulty in trusting others, a tendency toward re-victimization, substance abuse, and sexual maladjustment."[32] While this information provides a glimpse of what happens to survivors, it still only scratches the surface. The suffering can be overwhelming, even debilitating to the point of completely controlling their lives for years into adulthood. Many survivors also report thoughts and attempts of suicide. Because of this, we may never know the percentage of suicides caused by child sexual abuse.

---

32 Browne, Angela; Finkelhor, David. Psychological Bulletin, Vol 99(1), Jan 1986, 66-77. http://psycnet.apa.org/?fa=main.doiLanding&doi=10.1037/0033-2909.99.1.66

For Further Reflection

1. What possible consequences would make it difficult for you to speak up about child sexual abuse?

_____

_____

2. How can you be a part of a vigilant society?

_____

_____

DEVELOPING ENVIRONMENTS THAT PROMOTE DISCLOSURE

In a recovery guide for survivors of sexual abuse, the author lists what they termed a "Bill of Rights." Among them are the following truths:

(1) You have the right to be believed

(2) You have the right to be treated with dignity and respect

(3) You have the right to get help and support from others

(4) You have the right to heal.

We believe that any environment that promotes disclosure will be sensitive to and support these rights – especially for children. While we understand that this isn't always possible due to a wide range of circumstances, we believe that every effort must be made to ensure that survivors are not further traumatized or victimized in the process of disclosure whether in the home or in the child protection, law enforcement or legal environment.

While it is quite difficult tracking down methods or studies regarding developing environments that promote disclosure, we can learn a great deal from the statements of survivors who were traumatized in their disclosure process or found it increasingly difficult to disclose further after initially opening up. By taking a closer look at their experiences in different environments, we can see areas where change is needed.

In this example, a survivor of child sexual abuse recalls his disclosure of sexual abuse to his mother:

> I just described to her what he did to me one day (long pause) and she just told me to stay away from him. She said that if I really didn't like it that I should stop him.[33]

In this example, a survivor disclosed in a school setting at the age of seven:

> Then the teacher found out and I was told to go to the principal's office. At the principal's office, we didn't have a telephone, my mom and dad and I ended up with my grandmother finding out and she locked me up for two weeks, saying I was lying and I was terrible and I was telling all of these lies.[34]

These examples are not uncommon. There are countless instances in which children disclose in environments where adults are not prepared to properly relate with them. As a result, children who do disclose may never again do so following that experience.

Staller and Nelson-Gardell wrote:

> "For professionals working in the area of child sexual abuse (including police officers, lawyers, protective services workers, judges and social workers) it would be easier if children affirmatively disclosed abuse to a responsible adult in a trustworthy, detailed, consistent, and unwavering fashion (and better still if they could provide corroborating evidence to bolster their credibility). Authorities could assess the credibility of children, punish or treat offenders expediently, and intervene to effectively promote safety and recovery.
>
> In the real world, however, the disclosure process is neither so complete nor so linear. Children delay, partially disclose, retract, affirmatively disclose, accidentally disclose, recant, and reaffirm. Furthermore, ostensibly responsible adults can act unpredictably. They can discredit, denounce, challenge, threaten, and disbelieve. In short, the path of disclosure can be bumpy."[35]

---

[33] Alaggia, R. (2010). An ecological analysis of child sexual abuse disclosure: Considerations for child and adolescent mental health. *Journal of the Canadian Academy of Child and Adolescent Psychiatry, 19*(1), 35.
[34] Ibid, 35-36.
[35] Karen M. Staller, Debra Nelson-Gardell, "A burden in your heart": Lessons of disclosure from female preadolescent and adolescent survivors of sexual abuse, Child Abuse & Neglect, Volume 29, Issue 12, December 2005, Pages 1415-1432, ISSN 0145-2134, 10.1016/j.chiabu.2005.06.007. (http://www.sciencedirect.com/science/article/pii/S0145213405002577) Keywords: Sexual abuse; Disclosure; Qualitative methods; CSAAS

GAINING THE COURAGE TO SPEAK

Gaining the *Courage to Speak* out about this atrocity means overcoming all the fears and liabilities associated with child sexual abuse. We have covered many of these areas in this resource. We do, however, want to reiterate the importance of breaking the silence of child sexual abuse and creating an environment in which victims can speak.

For example, Angela's Voice recently contacted hundreds of faith centers across Georgia to encourage them to teach child sexual abuse prevention within their congregations and to offer programs that facilitate healing. The truth is, only a handful of those faith centers, showed any interest in facilitating awareness, prevention and healing programs. Yet, these organizations are among the most strategic and influential – outside of our homes and the educational system – to raise awareness and reach the most vulnerable population among us. Organizations like faith centers are also among the most likely places that predators can hide and gain easy access to our children.

Remember, 93 percent of all child sexual abuse is committed by people our children know and trust. In addition, faith-based organizations are uniquely positioned to be one of the most powerful voices in this fight due to their ability to impact children, families and communities. While time is spent talking about faith-based organizations here, I urge you to consider other organizations and groups that play a key role in this area.

Angela's Voice promotes awareness programs, like *Courage to Speak*, to raise the level of consciousness to such a degree as to force action to get the education necessary to protect a child. One workshop, one program, one 30-second PSA is not enough to ensure that you are vigilantly trained to protect a child. Angela's Voice promotes a menu of educational trainings on how to predict and prevent child sexual abuse.

The cycle of child sexual abuse can't be broken with prevention training alone. This is why Angela's Voice promotes healing programs in community so adult survivors of child sexual abuse have aftercare resources to process their pain and go on to live productive, peaceful and healthy lives. Every person in every segment of our society plays a key role in giving OUR SOCIETY the *Courage To Speak*.

Professional counseling is not enough and some survivors are even too stubborn to seek professional counseling because of the stigma associated with mental health, their lack of confidence in mental health profession, or the cost of treatment. This in fact is an even more important reason to have accessible aftercare for survivors. What does aftercare look like? Angela's Voice currently provides healing workshops, support groups and retreats for survivors. This is just a beginning of recognizing and responding responsibly to the pain and trauma a survivor suffers. **The more our society has the COURAGE TO SPEAK about this silenced taboo, the more permission will be transferred to survivors to gain THE COURAGE TO SPEAK.**

There is potentially the most important piece of prevention. If we can support the disclosure of child sexual abuse by adults, we end the pattern of abuse of that perpetrator to the next victim. On average, a perpetrator has 117 victims. If we can encourage children to disclose at a young age, we have just intercepted the next 116 before they become victims. If we can promote the disclosure of adults who are suffering from depression, addiction, cutting, eating disorders and other issues, we can help them find healing. They can have not only a healthier life but also experience them the opportunity to be a more healthy mother, father, sister, friend, teacher, coach, mentor or friend. The cycle can be broken but only with the COURAGE TO SPEAK to break the silence.

> For Further Reflection
>
> 1. How can you be part of creating an environment that promotes disclosure in your circle of influence?
>
> _____
>
> _____
>
> _____

CELEBRATING DISCLOSURE

Our culture has to learn how to have great compassion for survivors of child sexual abuse and nurture them back to healing. When your best friend tells you they have cancer, you hug them, cry with them, send them a card, bake them a casserole, ask if you can take them to the doctor, bring them a book on antioxidants, offer to clean their house, or care for their children. In turn, that best friend feels love, compassion and understanding of their fears and insecurities. If that same friend shared they were sexually abused for 6 years by their brother, you say, "Oh, that's awful! Why didn't you ever tell anyone?" The friend in turn looks inward, having now to explain all the conundrum of emotions and clams up for now and possibly forever.

Angela Williams of Angela's Voice explains, *"I have told my story of 14 years of child sexual abuse for years to thousands of people, including dozens of family members and received one letter from a removed relative explaining how sorry she was that my childhood was lost to abuse. During my time of full disclosure and healing, there was not a safe place to talk about my abuse. Family, work, friends, church; no place. I have received comments such as 'That is so gross; how can you talk about that; so why didn't you tell; you are destroying your mother by telling her dirty laundry; that is just too sad for people to hear."* Comments and attitudes like these silence victims.

So if you are a survivor who is reading *Courage to Speak*, we need your VOICE in the movement, a grassroots movement that is unified and organized to promote awareness, prevention and healing across our land. It is only by the disclosures of those who have experienced this trauma that we can truly come together as a society that says "No more!" Victory comes in taking your life back from abuse, receiving your VOICE, removing the shame and letting your story be heard loudly and boldly so that your story can give courage for the next story to be told. There are many impacted by the collateral damage of child sexual abuse that need to amplify their VOICE in the movement. The COURAGE TO SPEAK openly and honestly about this issue can and will save the next generation of children from child sexual abuse.

ANGELA'S VOICE

Angela's Voice is dedicated to developing, distributing, and endorsing valuable resources in the awareness, prevention, and healing of child sexual abuse. The materials, though specific for survivors of child sexual abuse, also benefit any abuse survivor and help protect children by teaching them how to defend themselves from abusive behavior. Founder Angela Williams, MFP, is a survivor-turned-advocate who shares a powerful message of triumph over tragedy by sharing her vulnerable and candid voice about her abuse trauma, her pain, her struggles, and her journey to healing in hopes that it may help other survivors expedite their healing journey.

Williams has devoted years to providing awareness, prevention, and healing programs through her advocacy work. Williams has captivated audiences with her powerful message of triumph over tragedy as a victim of childhood physical and sexual abuse. At age seventeen, she attempted suicide, and that day was the end of her torment and the beginning of a journey to healing. She is a crusader for change and dedicates her life to eradicate child sexual abuse. She holds a master's in forensic psychology with a concentration in child abuse. Williams is a powerful messenger, appearing in national and international news and documentaries. She has been successful in state legislative reform and national policy work and served on the Policy Committee of the National Coalition to Prevent Child Sexual Abuse and Exploitation. She has received numerous accolades and awards for her work, including her collection of books that have valuable lessons for survivors of all ages.

Please follow Angela Williams on social media and contact angelasvoice.com to book a speaking event or interview.

Books by Angela Williams

Loving Me: After Abuse
From Sorrows to Sapphires, Angela Williams's Memoir

Interactive Workbooks—Adults

<u>Healing</u>
Pathway to Healing, Guide to Healing
True Intimacy
Shattering the Shame
Unveiling Child Sexual Abuse

<u>Prevention</u>
Tough Talk to Tender Hearts
The Grooming Mystery
Single Parenting Solutions
Courage to Speak

Children's Books (Ages 5–10)
Gracie Finds Her Voice
Grant Gets His Shield
Gracie and Grant's Big Win
Gracie and Grant's Big Win Coloring Book
Find Your Voice Curriculum Book

Join the Angela's Voice Movement

Take action to break the silence and cycle of Child Sexual Abuse and Exploitation

HELP US SAVE THE NEXT GENERATION OF CHILDREN!

1. Be a Child Advocate
2. Donate at angelasvoice.com
3. Invite Angela Williams to Speak
4. Purchase another Angela's Voice Prevention or Healing Book

Discover more child sexual abuse prevention and healing resources at angelasvoice.com and follow angelasvoice in social media.

Instagram @Angelasvoice

Facebook @Angelasvoice

Twitter @Angelasvoice

Linkedin/angelasvoice

Angelasvoice.blogspot.com

Youtube.com/angelakwilliams